Place your photo here

All About Me

Full name

Date of birth

Confirmation name

Date of Baptism

Date of First Holy Communion

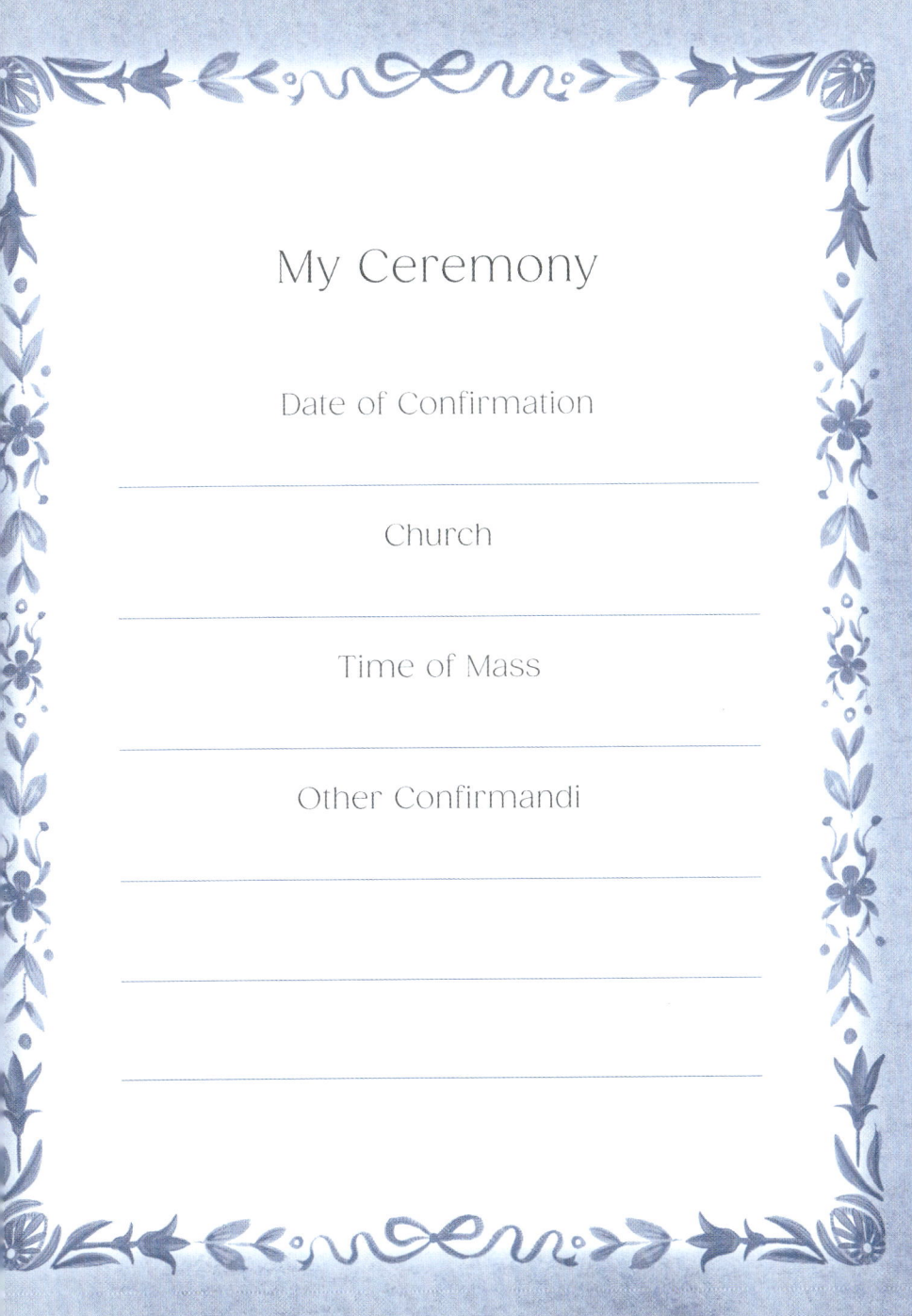

My Ceremony

Date of Confirmation

_____

Church

_____

Time of Mass

_____

Other Confirmandi

_____

_____

_____

My Ceremony

Special moments

_____

_____

Readings chosen

_____

Who proclaimed the readings

_____

What is Confirmation?

At confirmation, a person takes on the promises that their godparents made for them at their baptism. They now make those promises their own, and choose to follow Jesus Christ for the rest of their lives.

A bishop anoints them and prays for them to be filled with the Holy Spirit. From now on, that person does their best, with the help of the Holy Spirit, to reject sin and evil and to walk in the way of Christ.

My Confirmation

Place your photo here

Place your photo here

My Testimony

Rite of Confirmation

"Be sealed with the Gift of the Holy Spirit."

My Saint or Bible Character

Some people choose a Saint,

or someone from the Bible,

as their own example to think

and pray about when

they get confirmed.

My Saint or Bible character

_____

_____

Why I've chosen this person to look up to

_____

_____

Their special virtues

_____

_____

How I hope to follow their example

_____

_____

My role in the church

My ministry interests

_____

_____

_____

How I can give back to the church

_____

_____

_____

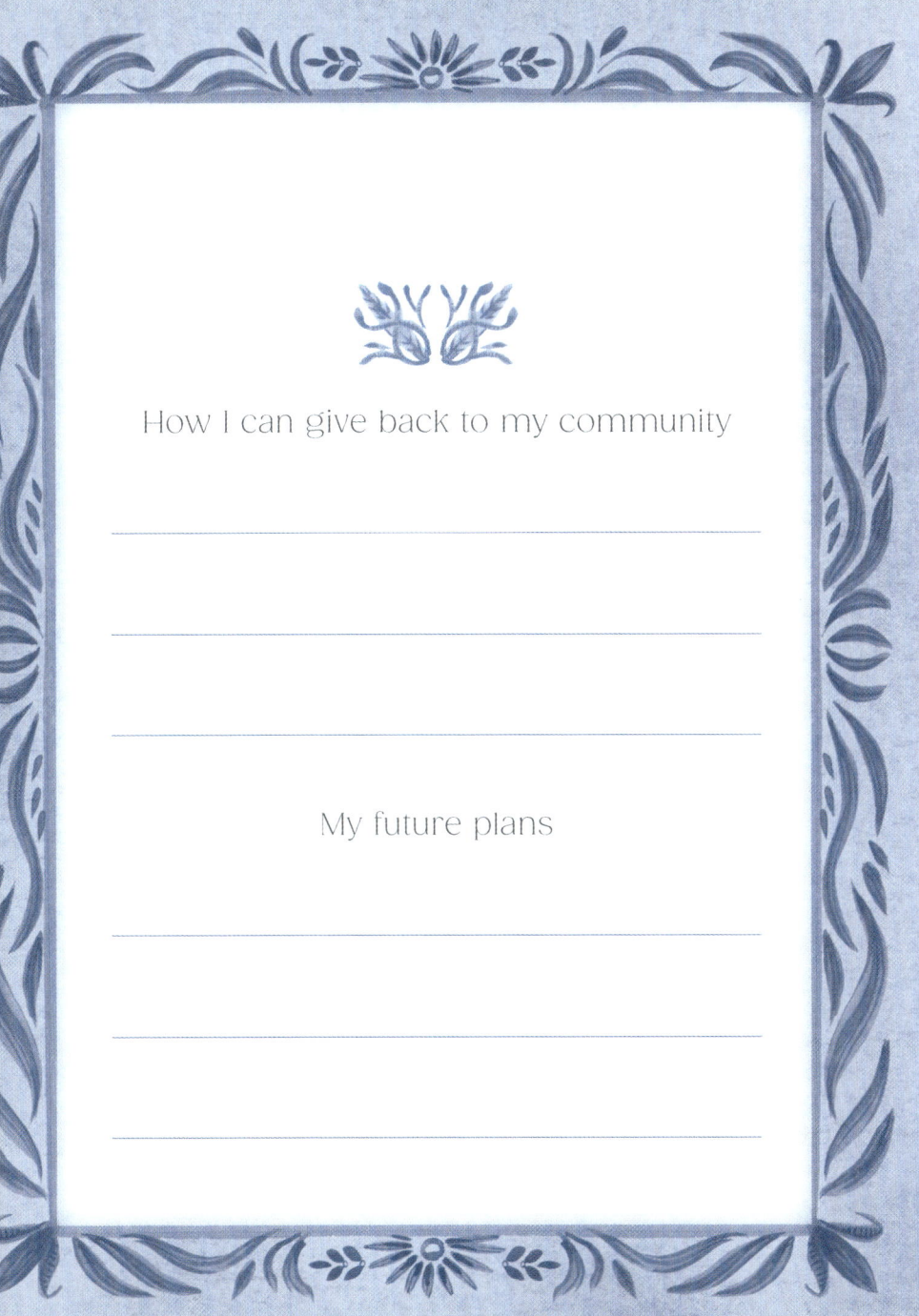

How I can give back to my community

My future plans

The Seven Gifts

The LORD's Spirit will rest on him: the spirit of wisdom and understanding, the spirit of counsel and might, the spirit of knowledge and of the fear of the LORD. His delight will be in the fear of the LORD. He will not judge by the sight of his eyes, neither decide by the hearing of his ears;

but he will judge the poor with righteousness, and decide with equity for the humble of the earth. He will strike the earth with the rod of his mouth; and with the breath of his lips he will kill the wicked. Righteousness will be the belt around his waist, and faithfulness the belt around his waist.

(Isaiah 11:2-5)

Gifts of the Holy Spirit reflection

Wisdom
How I hope to use this gift

_____

_____

_____

Understanding
My prayer for deeper faith

_____

_____

_____

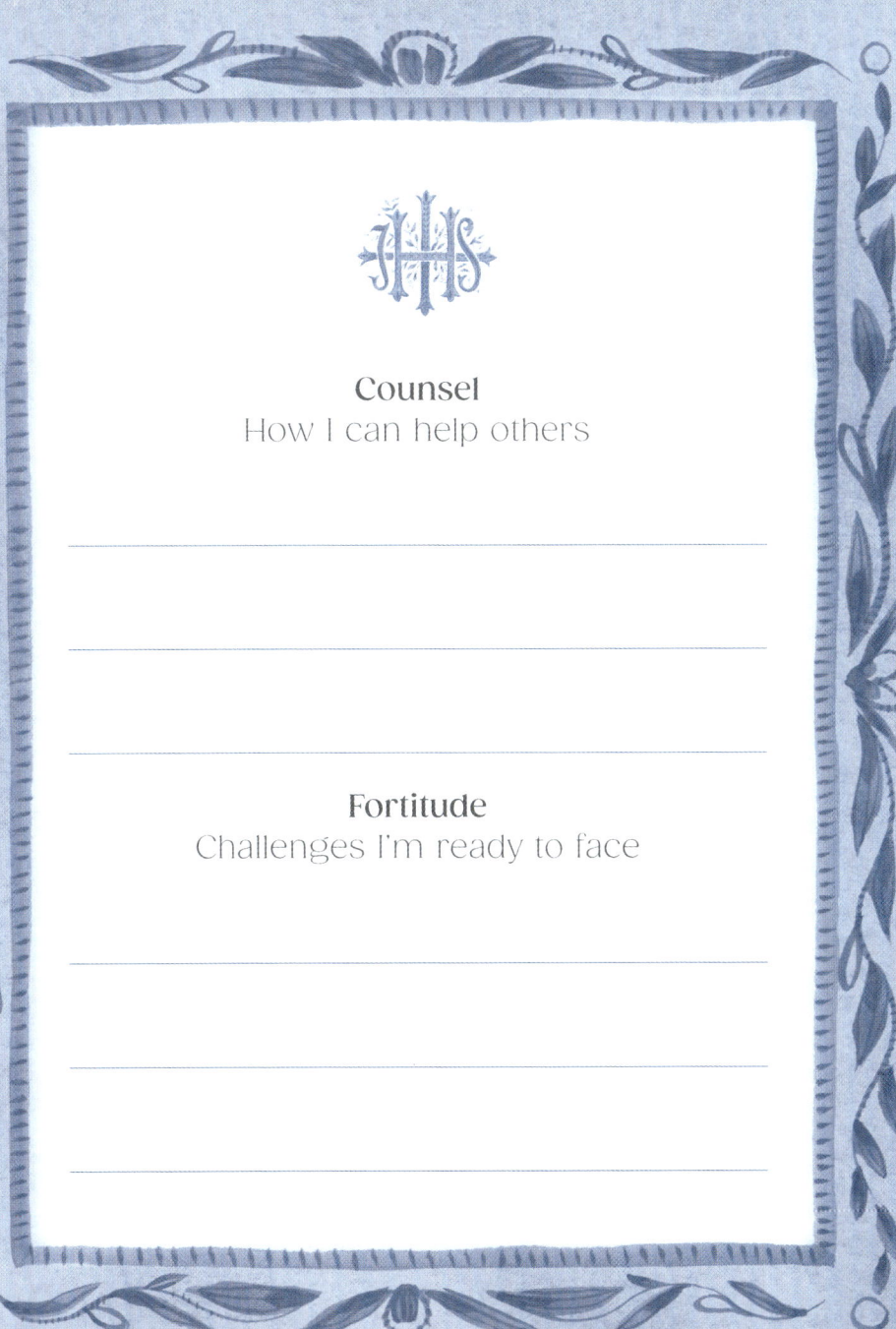

Counsel
How I can help others

_____

_____

_____

Fortitude
Challenges I'm ready to face

_____

_____

_____

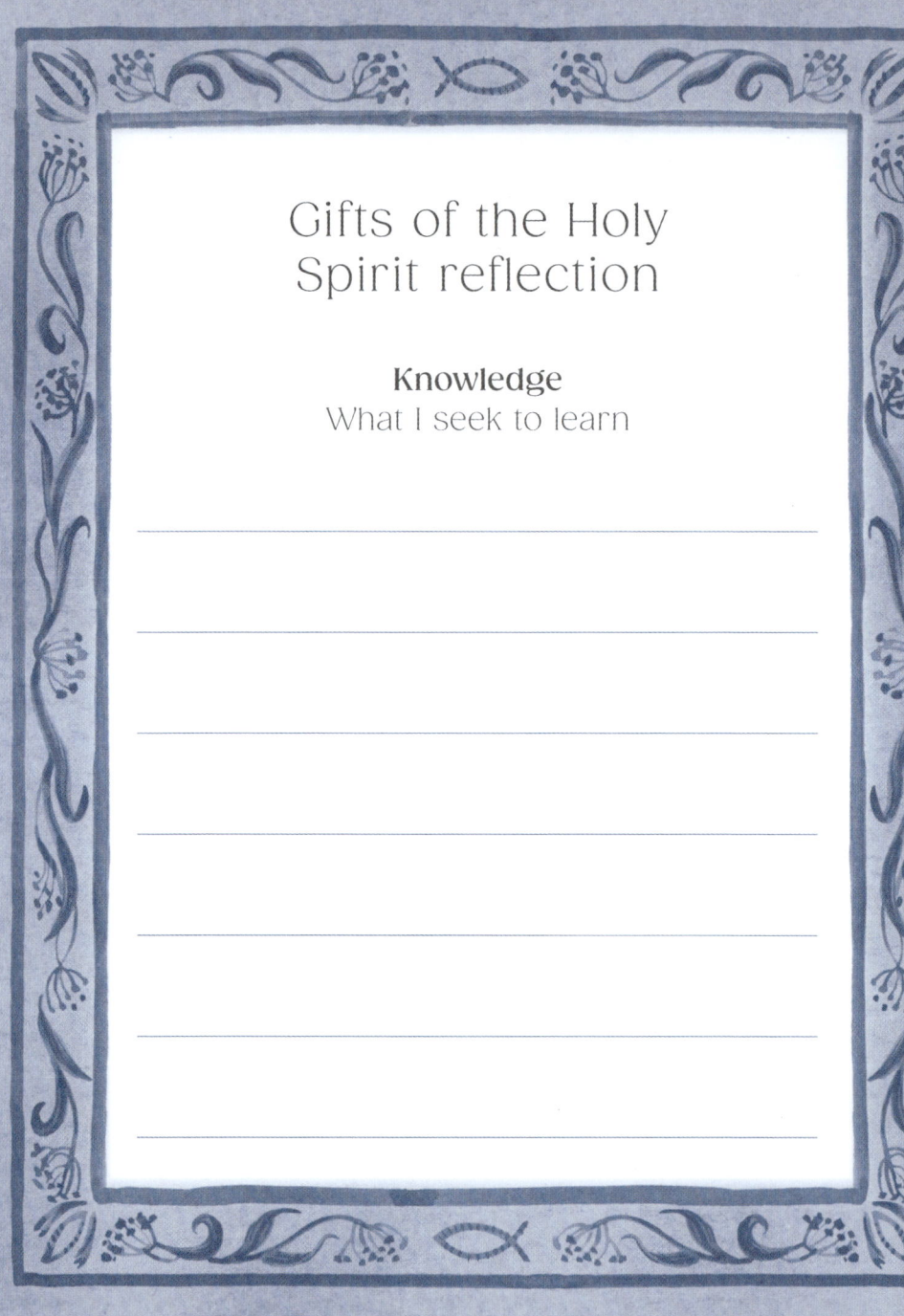

Gifts of the Holy Spirit reflection

Knowledge
What I seek to learn

Piety
How I will deepen my devotion

Fear of the Lord
My commitment to God

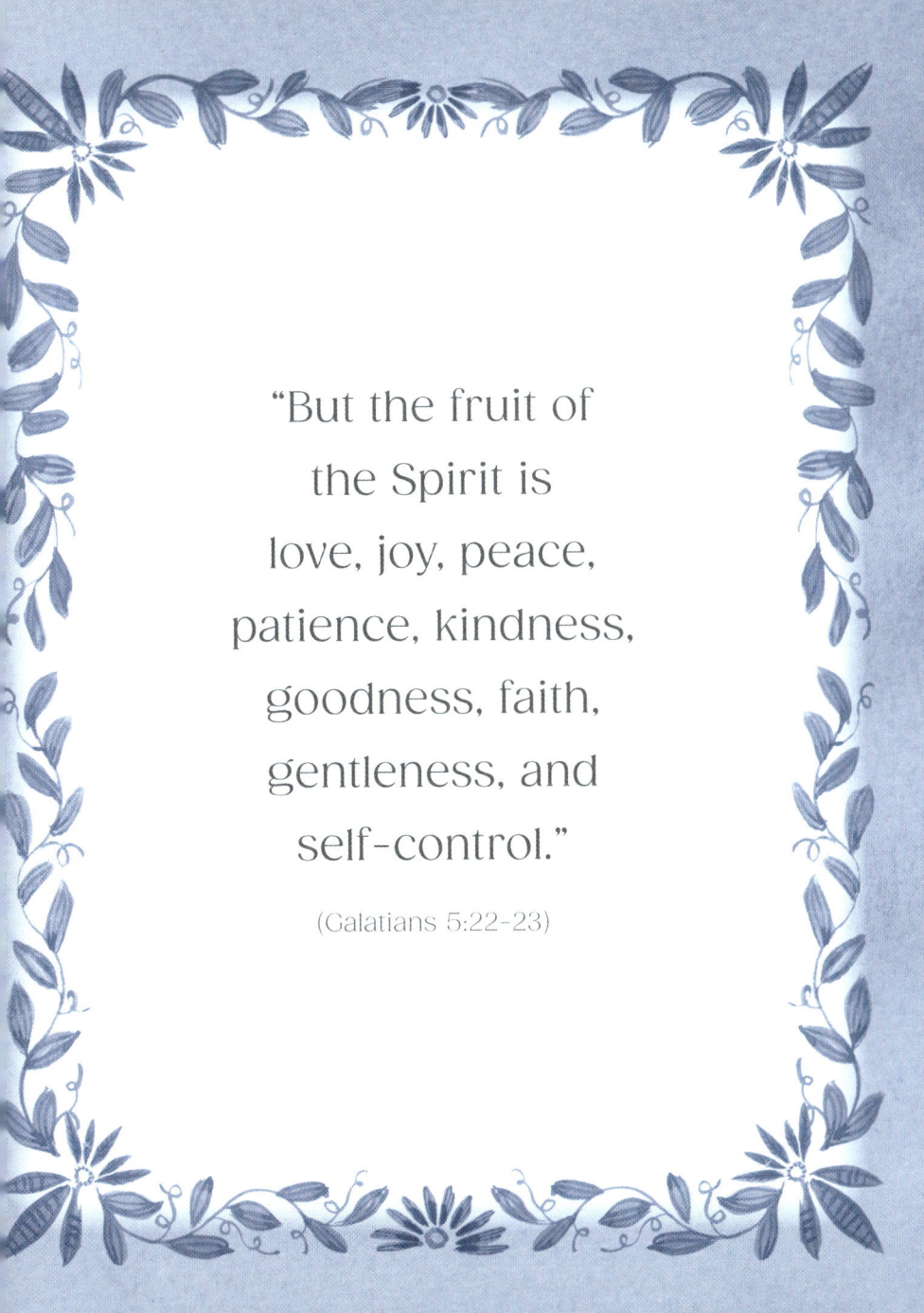

"But the fruit of the Spirit is love, joy, peace, patience, kindness, goodness, faith, gentleness, and self-control."

(Galatians 5:22-23)

My favourite hymns

What they mean to me

Gifts given to me on my special day

_____

_____

_____

_____

_____

_____

_____

"'But you will receive power when the Holy Spirit has come upon you.

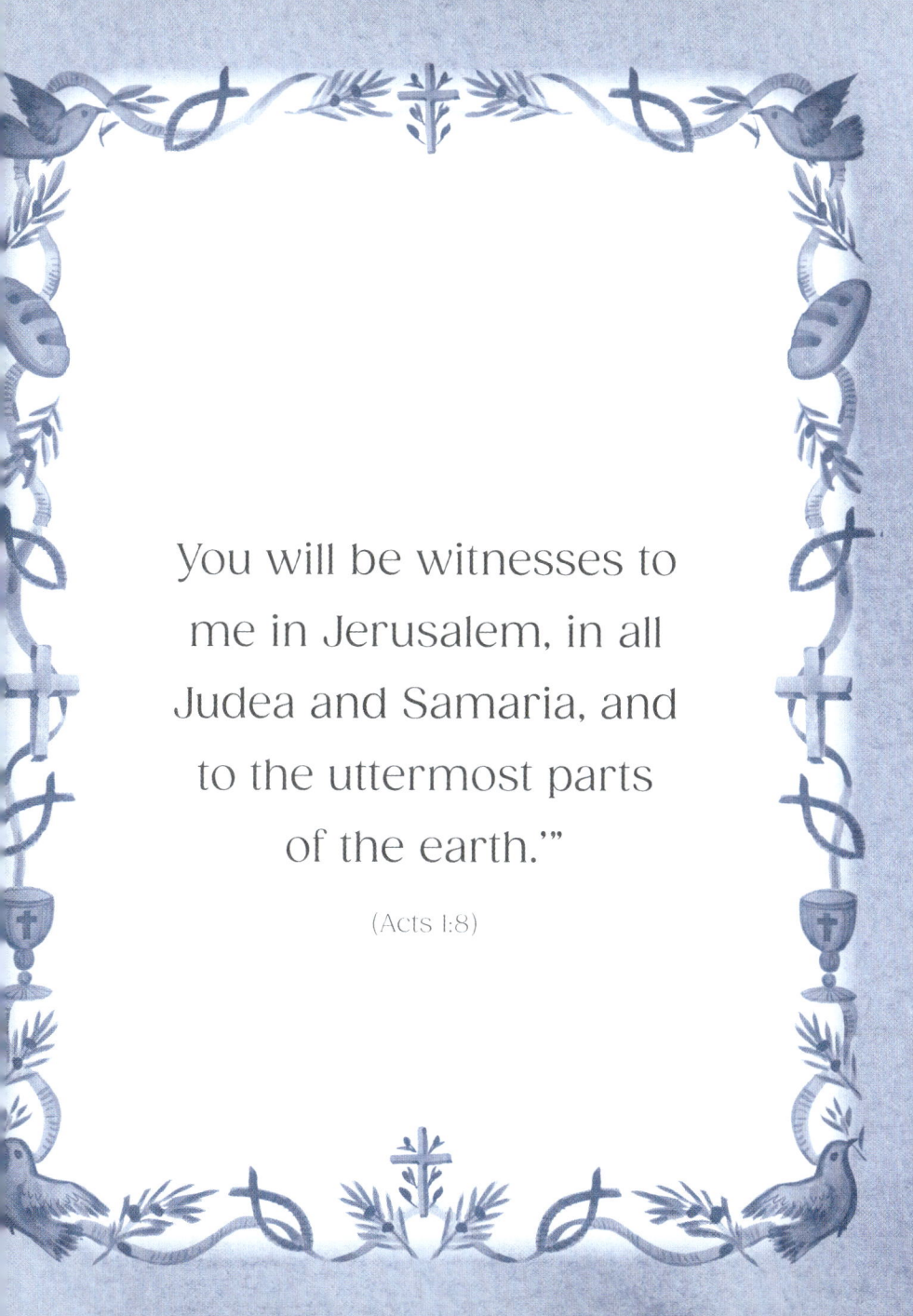

You will be witnesses to me in Jerusalem, in all Judea and Samaria, and to the uttermost parts of the earth.'"

(Acts 1:8)

My Faith Commitments

Ways I will share my faith

_____

_____

Ways I will nurture my faith

_____

_____

My spiritual goals for the future

The Pilgrimage

By Sir Walter Raleigh

Give me my scallop shell of quiet,

My staff of faith to walk upon,

My scrip of joy, immortal diet,

My bottle of salvation,

My gown of glory, hope's true gage,

And thus I'll take my pilgrimage.

A letter for the future

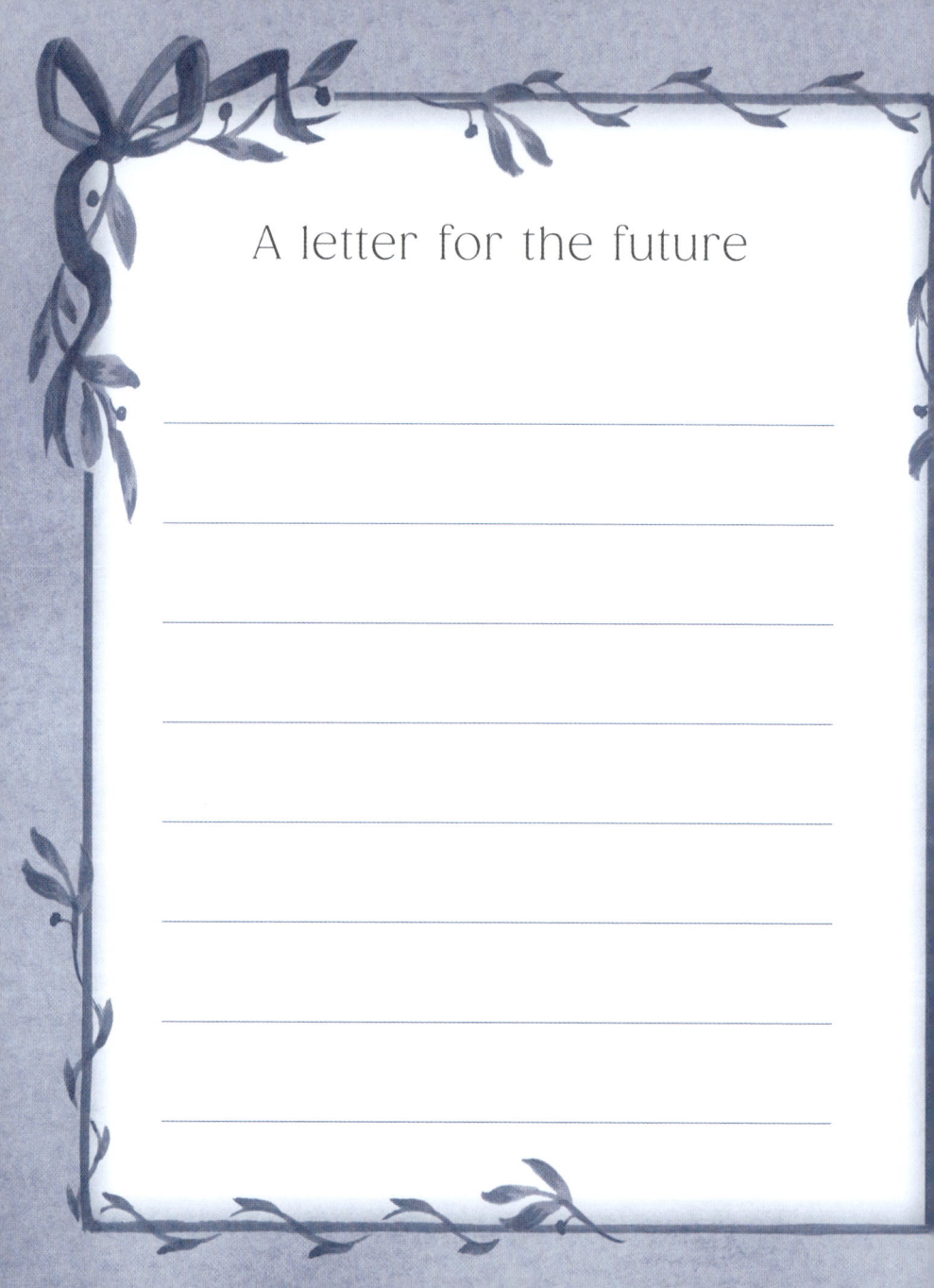

Scriptures to turn to in times of need

Sad

"'Come to me, all you who labor and are heavily burdened, and I will give you rest. Take my yoke upon you and learn from me, for I am gentle and humble in heart; and you will find rest for your souls. For my yoke is easy, and my burden is light.'"

(Matthew 11:28-30)

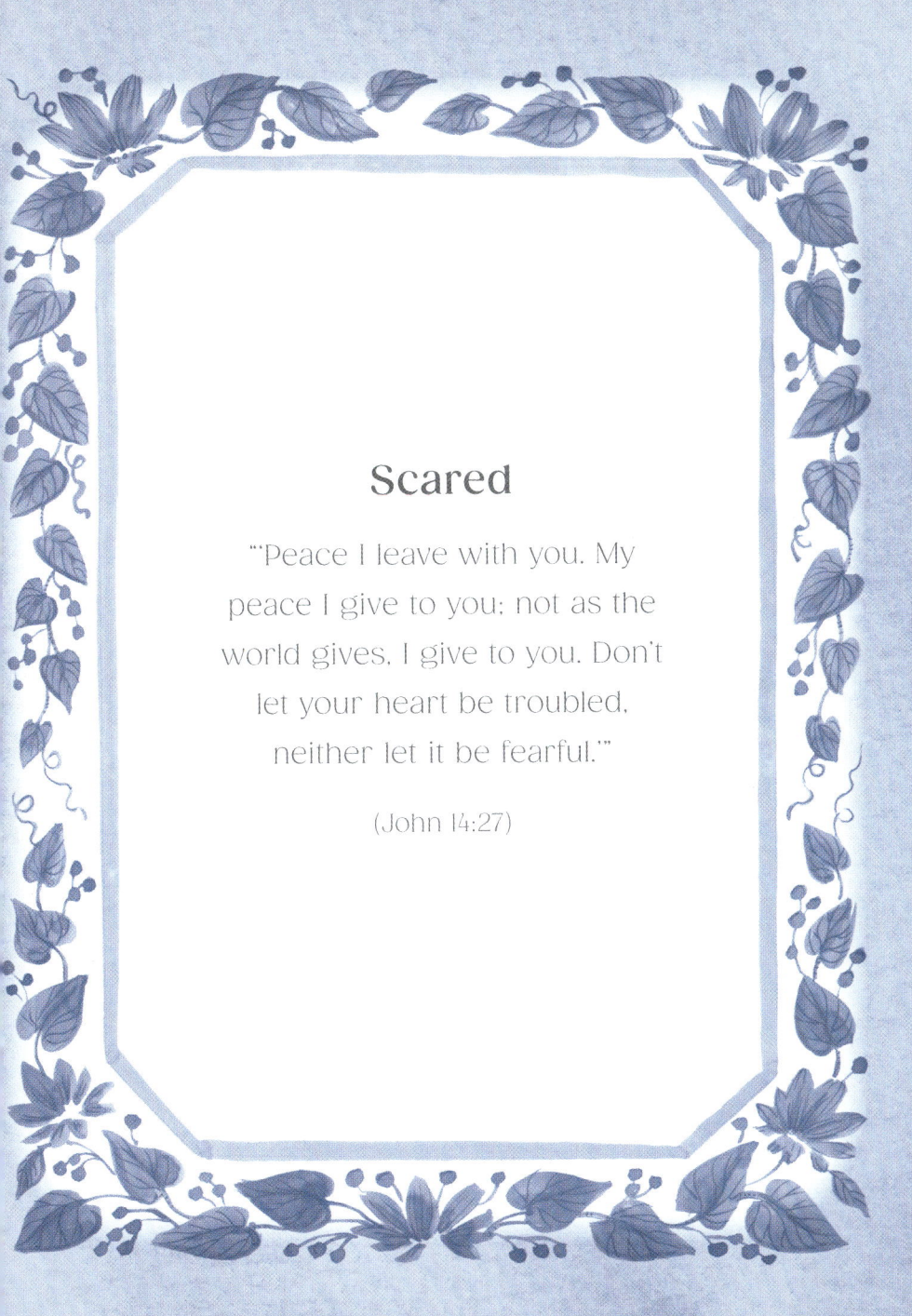

Scared

"'Peace I leave with you. My peace I give to you; not as the world gives, I give to you. Don't let your heart be troubled, neither let it be fearful.'"

(John 14:27)

Lonely

"'Behold, I am with you always,
even to the end of the age.'"

(Matthew 28:20)

Anxious

"Humble yourselves therefore
under the mighty hand of God,
that he may exalt you in due time,
casting all your worries on him,
because he cares for you."

(I Peter 5:6-7)

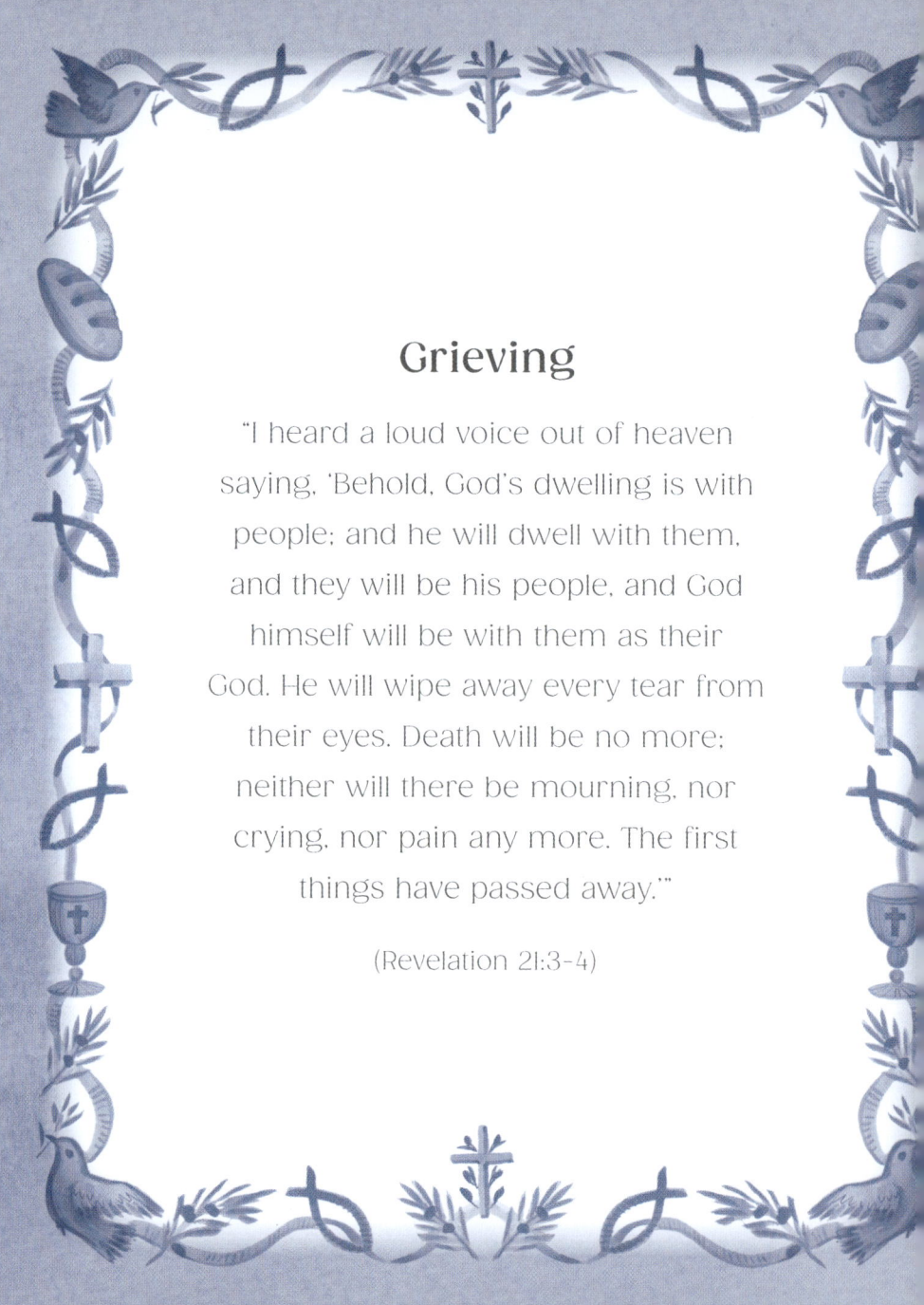

Grieving

"I heard a loud voice out of heaven saying, 'Behold, God's dwelling is with people; and he will dwell with them, and they will be his people, and God himself will be with them as their God. He will wipe away every tear from their eyes. Death will be no more; neither will there be mourning, nor crying, nor pain any more. The first things have passed away.'"

(Revelation 21:3-4)

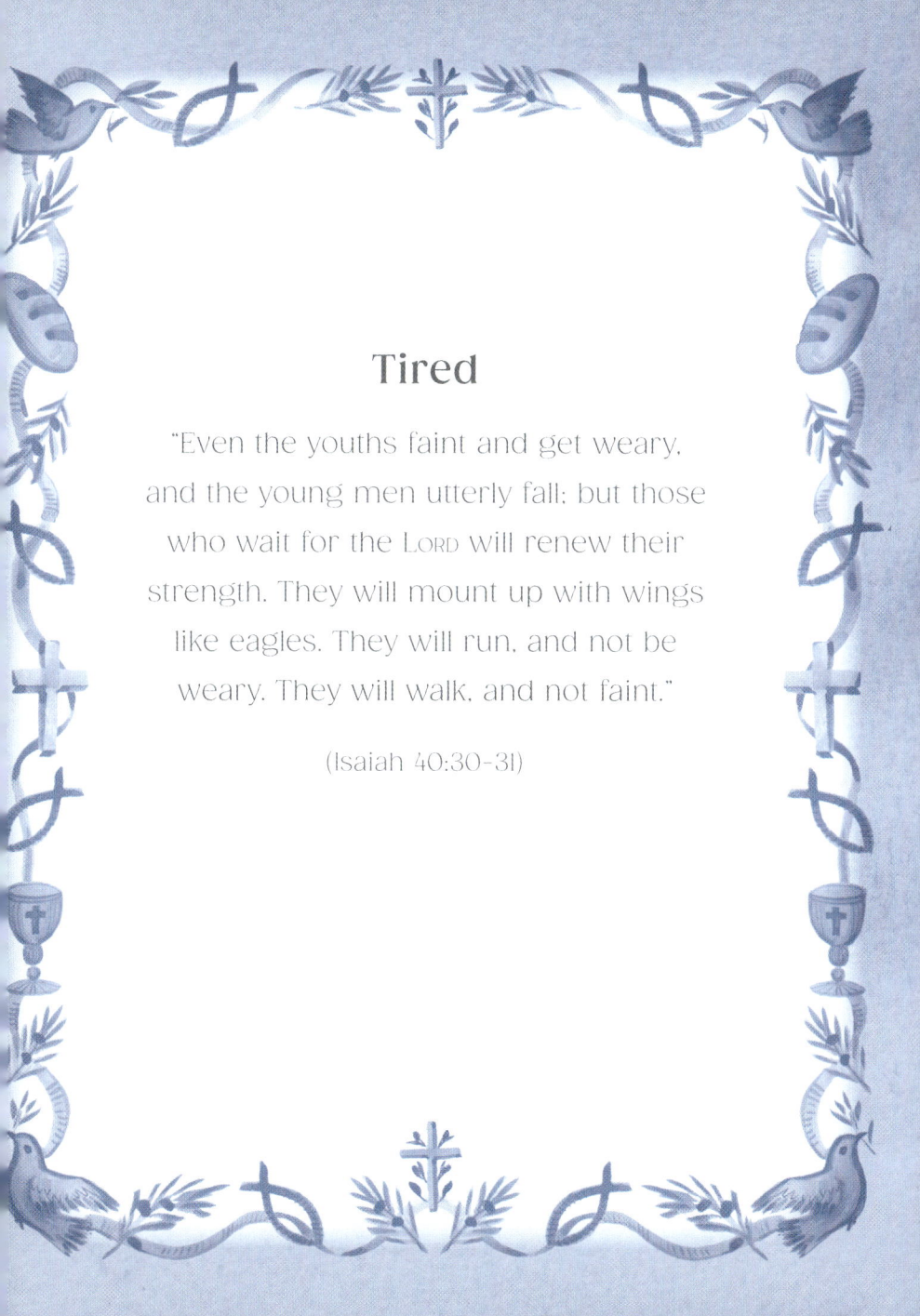

Tired

"Even the youths faint and get weary, and the young men utterly fall; but those who wait for the Lord will renew their strength. They will mount up with wings like eagles. They will run, and not be weary. They will walk, and not faint."

(Isaiah 40:30-31)

Thankful

"Give thanks to the Lord, for he is good, for his loving kindness endures forever."

(Psalms 118:1)

Small

"Let no man despise your youth; but be an example to those who believe, in word, in your way of life, in love, in spirit, in faith, and in purity."

(1 Timothy 4:12)

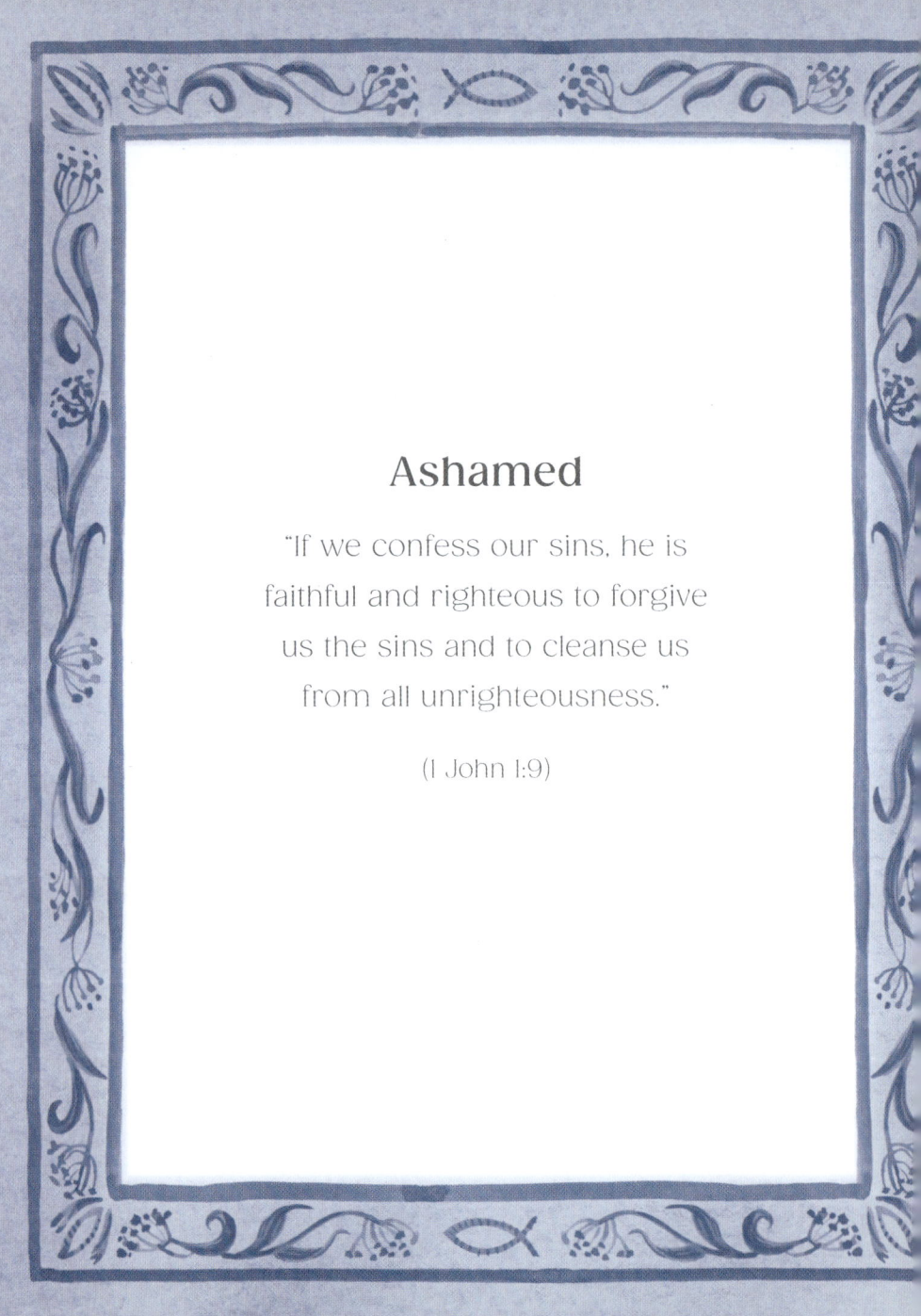

Ashamed

"If we confess our sins, he is faithful and righteous to forgive us the sins and to cleanse us from all unrighteousness."

(1 John 1:9)

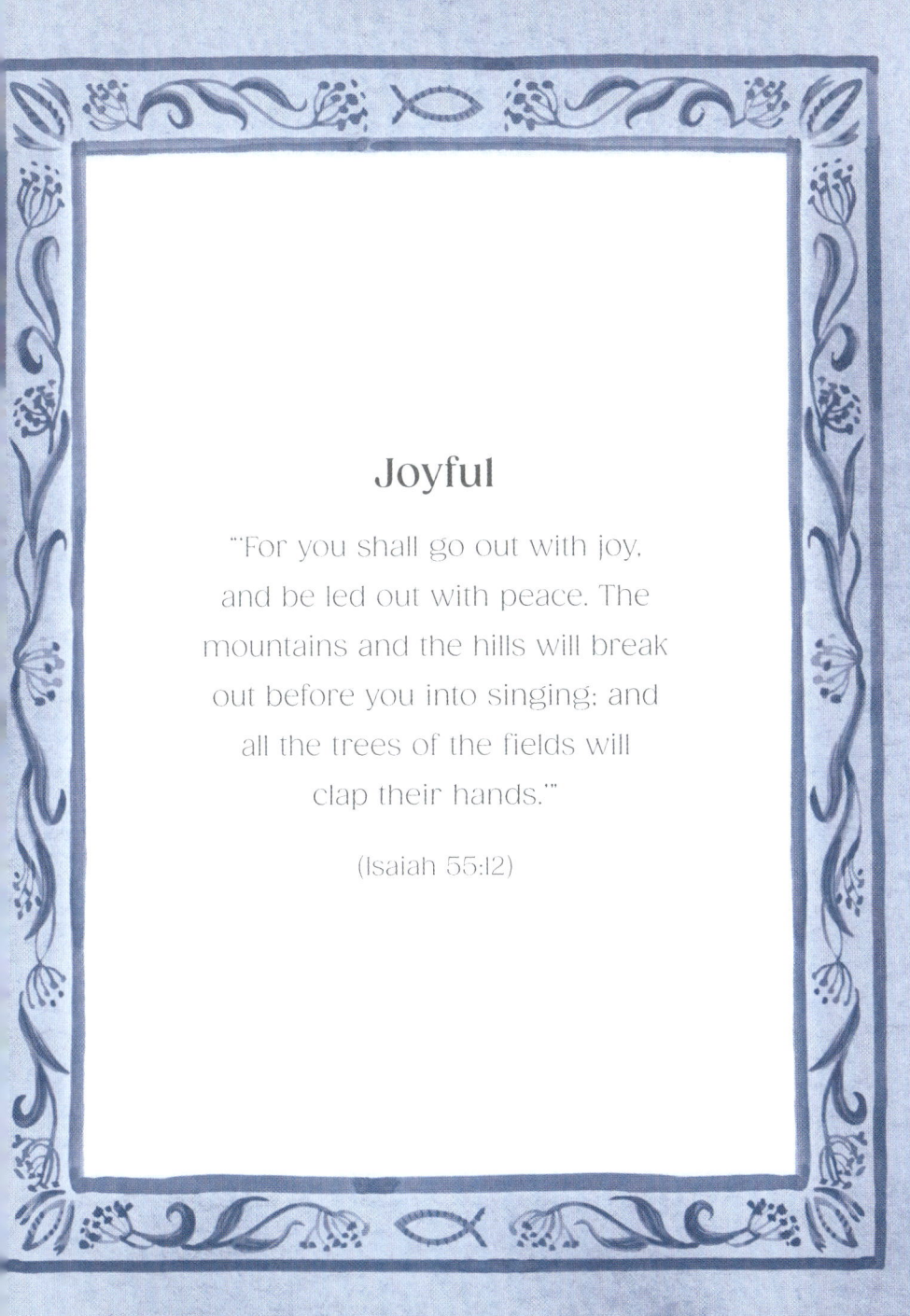

Joyful

"'For you shall go out with joy,
and be led out with peace. The
mountains and the hills will break
out before you into singing; and
all the trees of the fields will
clap their hands.'"

(Isaiah 55:12)

Reflections

1 year on from my Confirmation

_____

_____

My achievements

_____

_____

I am working towards

_____

_____

My goals for the future

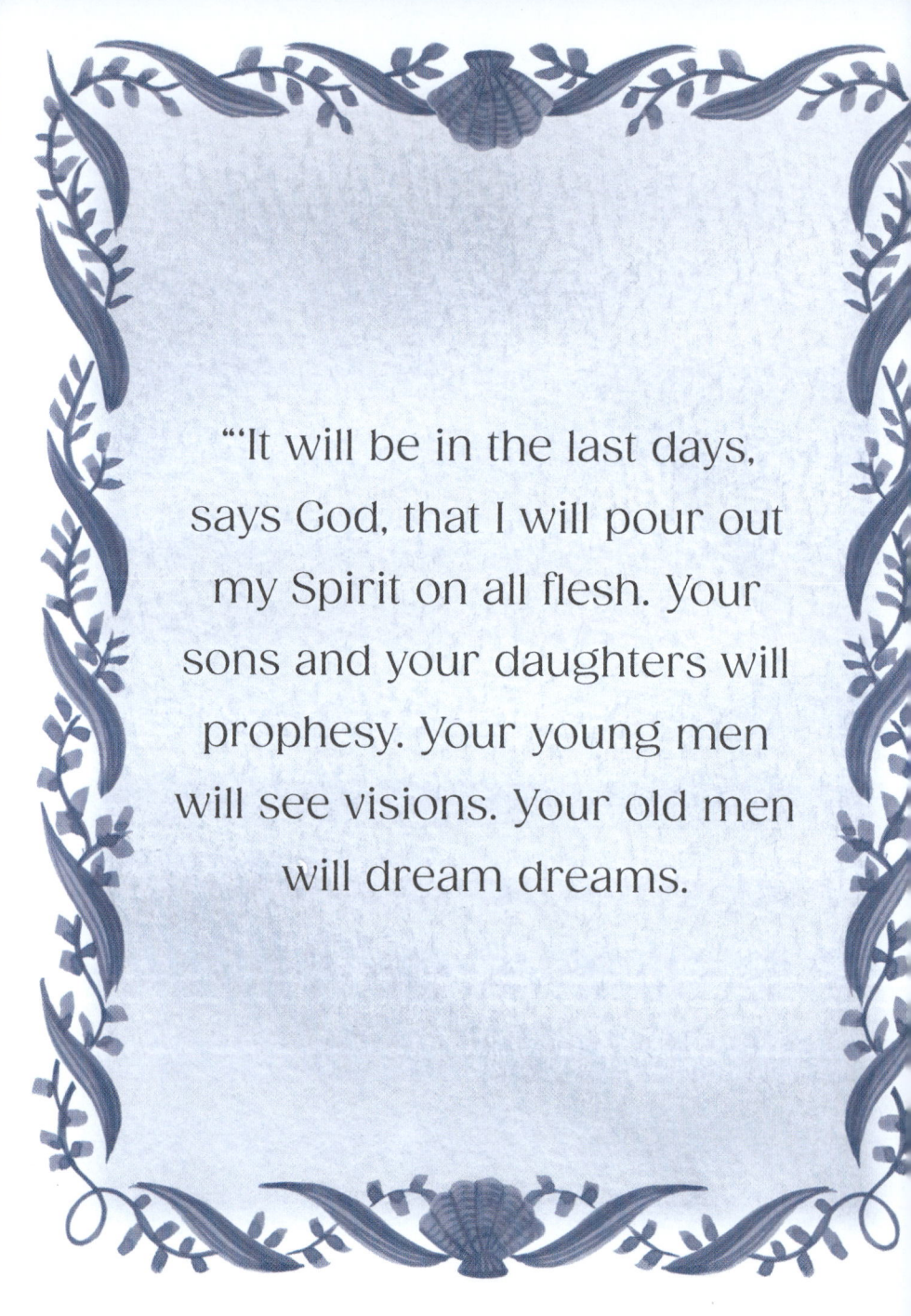

"'It will be in the last days, says God, that I will pour out my Spirit on all flesh. Your sons and your daughters will prophesy. Your young men will see visions. Your old men will dream dreams.

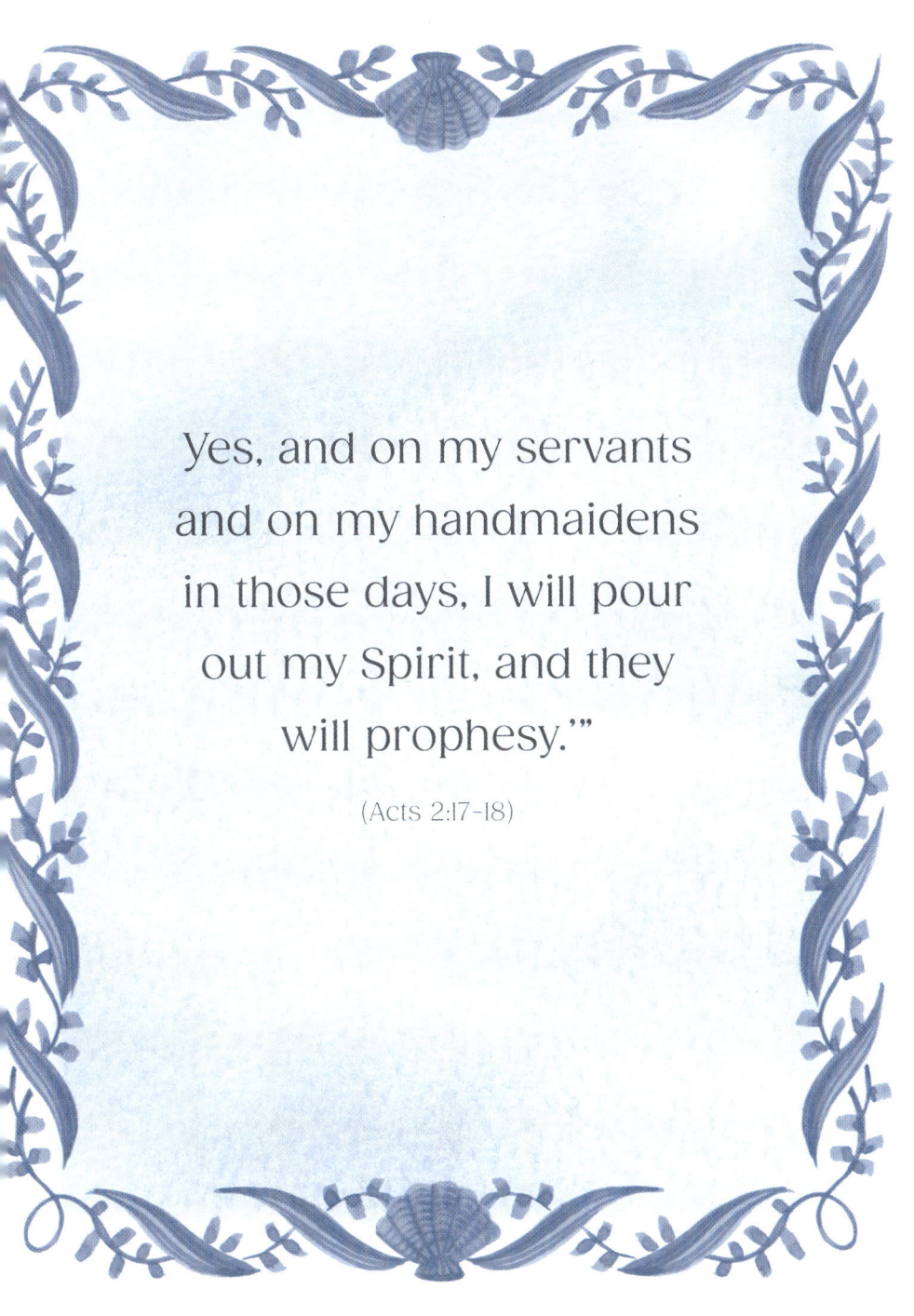

Yes, and on my servants and on my handmaidens in those days, I will pour out my Spirit, and they will prophesy.'"

(Acts 2:17-18)

Thoughts, hopes, and messages

from those who matter most

Thoughts, hopes, and messages

from those who matter most

Thoughts, hopes, and messages

from those who matter most

Thoughts, hopes, and messages

Thoughts, hopes, and messages

_____

_____

_____

_____

_____

_____

_____

from those who matter most

Thoughts, hopes, and messages

from those who matter most

Thoughts, hopes, and messages

from those who matter most

Thoughts, hopes, and messages

from those who matter most

Thoughts, hopes, and messages

from those who matter most

Place your photo here

Place your photo here

Place your photo here

DK | Penguin Random House

Illustrated by Victoria Nelson

First published in Great Britain in 2026 by
Dorling Kindersley Limited
20 Vauxhall Bridge Road,
London SW1V 2SA

The authorised representative in the EEA is
Dorling Kindersley Verlag GmbH. Arnulfstr. 124,
80636 Munich, Germany

Copyright © 2026 Dorling Kindersley Limited
A Penguin Random House Company
10 9 8 7 6 5 4 3 2 1
001–352582–Mar/2026

All Scripture quotations are taken from the
World English Bible (WEB)

All rights reserved.
No part of this publication may be reproduced, stored
in or introduced into a retrieval system, or transmitted,
in any form, or by any means (electronic, mechanical,
photocopying, recording, or otherwise), without the prior
written permission of the copyright owner.
No part of this publication may be used or reproduced in
any manner for the purpose of training artificial intelligence
technologies or systems. In accordance with Article 4(3) of
the DSM Directive 2019/790, DK expressly reserves this
work from the text and data mining exception.

A CIP catalogue record for this book
is available from the British Library.
ISBN: 978-0-2417-7114-3

Printed and bound in India

www.dk.com

MIX
Paper | Supporting
responsible forestry
FSC™ C018179

This book was made with Forest Stewardship Council™ certified paper – one small step in DK's commitment to a sustainable future.
Learn more at www.dk.com/uk/information/sustainability